T0016833

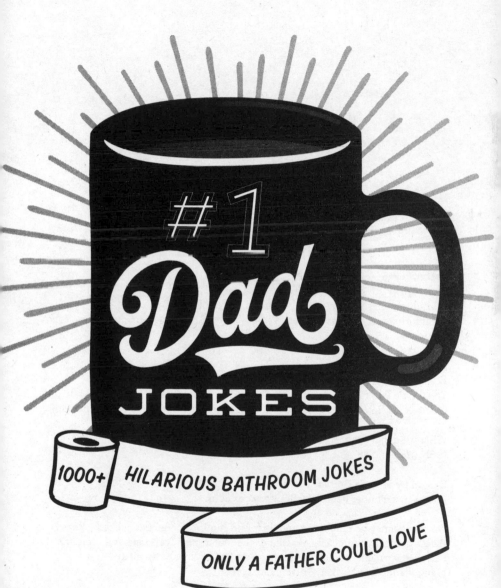

#1 Dad JOKES

1000+ HILARIOUS BATHROOM JOKES

ONLY A FATHER COULD LOVE

JERRY CARLIN

#1 Dad Jokes
Copyright © 2023 by St. Martin's Press.
All rights reserved. Printed in the United States of America.
For information, address St. Martin's Publishing Group, 120 Broadway, New York,
NY 10271.

www.castlepointbooks.com

The Castle Point Books trademark is owned by Castle Point Publishing, LLC.
Castle Point books are published and distributed by St. Martin's Publishing Group.

ISBN 978-1-250-28537-9 (trade paperback)
ISBN 978-1-250-28538-6 (ebook)

Design by Melissa Gerber
Images used under license by Shutterstock.com

Our books may be purchased in bulk for promotional, educational, or business use.
Please contact your local bookseller or the Macmillan Corporate and Premium
Sales Department at 1-800-221-7945, extension 5442, or by email at
MacmillanSpecialMarkets@macmillan.com.

First Edition: 2023

10 9 8 7 6 5 4 3 2 1

CONTENTS

Wise Cracks

PLUMBING
THE DEPTHS

What's on a roll but doesn't have any wheels?

Toilet paper.

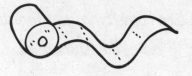

**What's the best name
for a plumber?**

Dwayne.

Two boys go into two bathroom stalls and finish at about the same time. The first boy goes to the sink to wash his hands. The second boy is about to leave, and the first boy asks, "Aren't you going to wash your hands? I was taught to always wash my hands after using the bathroom." The second boy laughed and said, "Well, I was taught not to pee on my hands," and he left.

**What kind of shoes do
plumbers hate the most?**

Clogs.

Real Movies

Real movies that sound like something you would do in the bathroom:

- *Splash*
- *Free Willy*
- *Fire Down Below*
- *What Lies Beneath*
- *That Thing You Do*
- *Unfinished Business*
- *Sudden Impact*
- *Peewee's Big Adventure*

What do you call going to the bathroom on an RV?

Going on the go!

Why shouldn't you take Pokémon into the bathroom when you need to go?

They might Pikachu.

Did you hear about the kid who had to give a report and hid in the bathroom?

He was stalling.

Knock-knock!

Who's there?

Noah.

Noah who?

Noah where the bathroom is? I'm about to blow!

Knock-knock!

Who's there?

Queen.

Queen who?

Queen the bathroom please.

How does a plumber stay fit?
He does plunges.

Where's the best place to buy toilet paper?
Just find it on Poo-gle.

Knock-knock!

Who's there?

Distinct.

Distinct who?

Distinct when you come out of the bathroom is disgusting.

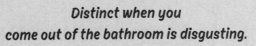

**What stinks,
is covered in mold,
and doesn't belong
in the bathroom?**

Cheese.

**Why did the cowboy have to
poop standing up?**

Because a cowboy should never squat
while wearing spurs.

**What is the worst air freshener
to have in the bathroom?**

Poo-pourri.

**Where do leprechauns
use the bathroom?**

In pots o' gold.

Did you hear about the man who would only bathe in the spring?

He was incredibly smelly because people should bathe in all seasons.

Why did Cleopatra lock the door when she went to the bathroom?

She was afraid someone would Caesar.

Knock-knock!

Who's there?

Fanny.

Fanny who?

Fanny'body knocks, tell them I'm going to be in here awhile.

TYPES OF POOP

- **_The Fruitcake:_** The sort of poop that's such an ordeal that you don't want to see it again for at least another year.

- **_Jaws:_** Things are quiet at first ... but then the tension starts to build. Better get outta the water, quick!

- **_The DMV:_** Clear your schedule because this one is going to take ALL DAY.

- **_The Scrubber:_** A poop so big that it cleans your hole on its way out.

- **_The Haunted Poop:_** When you go to the bathroom in the middle of the night and you're convinced something might be in the toilet.

- **_Mount Vesuvius:_** Unexpected—and dangerously explosive—diarrhea.

Knock-knock!
Who's there?
Arthur.
Arthur who?
Arthur any plumbers on duty?
'Cuz we're gonna need one!

**What did the toilet seat
say about the messy man?**

"It's so nice of him to
always leave something behind."

Why did the plumber quit his job?

He was tired of getting calls about
leaks in the bathroom.

Why did the plumber pee on his shoes?

He wanted to work from home.

Knock-knock!

Who's there?

Censure.

Censure who?

Censure so smart, why don't you show me
how to unclog the toilet?

What is the biggest mistake
a pirate can make
in the bathroom?

Wiping with the
wrong hand.

Knock-knock!

Who's there?

Hank.

Hank who?

Hank you for turning on the fan
in the bathroom!

Knock-knock!

Who's there?

Stopwatch.

Stopwatch who?

Stopwatch you're doing
and clean up this bathroom!

Knock-knock!

Who's there?

Abbott.

Abbott who?

Abbott time we got a candle
for this bathroom!

Knock-knock!

Who's there?

Dewey.

Dewey who?

Dewey really have to share
this bathroom?

What song does the Lone Ranger sing when he goes to the bathroom?

"Take a dump, take a dump, take a dump dump dump . . ."

Knock-knock!

Who's there?

Juicy.

Juicy who?

Juicy a plunger anywhere around here?

What does the queen do after she goes to the bathroom?

Makes a royal flush.

Knock-knock!

Who's there?

Madam.

Madam who?

Madam toilet won't flush!

License to Smell

*Some people love
bathroom humor so much
they have to take it
on the road!*

- LUV2FRT
- IFRTID
- IGOTTAP
- RNONGAS
- KSMYGAS
- OLDFRT
- PASNGAS
- ICUP
- LUVSHARTZ
- BUTKISR
- TURDLE
- DIDUFRT
- NVRFLSH
- BGDMP
- IHAVGAS
- H8FARTS
- GOT2POO
- JCYPOO

**What kind of toilets
can you buy at a drugstore?**

Toilet-trees.

Knock-knock!

Who's there?

Needle.

Needle who?

Needle little help
finding a bathroom?

**When is the most satisfying time
to go to the bathroom?**

Poo thirty!

Knock-knock!

Who's there?

Joanne.

Joanne who?

Joanne's need to get washed
after that bathroom visit.

Why did the woman put plastic wrap on the toilet seat?

She wanted to seal in the freshness.

Knock-knock!

Who's there?

Police.

Police who?

*Police open the door,
it's a bathroom emergency!*

Knock-knock!

Who's there?

Candice.

Candice who?

Candice bathroom smell any worse?

What do you call a bunch of strawberries clogging up a toilet?

A real jam.

TYPES OF POOP

- **The Ploop:** When you go and it makes a nice little splash!

- **The Cookout:** When there are visible chunks of corn in there.

- **The False Alarm:** When you rush to get to a bathroom only to discover it was just a fart.

- **The Dentist:** A poop that takes so long and hurts so much it's like pulling teeth.

- **The Hallelujah:** When you finally get to poop after being stuck in traffic for an hour and needing to use the bathroom the whole time.

- **The Viper:** A poop that coils so much that you fear it might strike back out of the toilet.

- **The Infomercial:** When you think you're done . . . but wait! There's more!

- **The Crayon:** When it leaves marks in the bowl even after you flush.

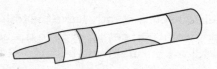

FOUL LANGUAGE

Even the most interesting people in history love to talk about what we do in the bathroom.

"Everybody looks at their poop." —OPRAH WINFREY

"Always go to the bathroom when you have a chance."
—KING GEORGE V

"Home is where the heart is, home is where the fart is."
—ERNEST HEMINGWAY

"Fart for freedom, fart for liberty—and fart proudly."
—BENJAMIN FRANKLIN

"An employer's fart is music to his employees' ears."
—MOKOKOMA MOKHONOANA

"You failed—your fart was not silent, my nose heard its deafening noise." —ANIEKEE TOCHUKWU EZEKIEL

"My trumpeting sounds like a goose farting in the fog."
—ALEX O'LOUGHLIN

"You are all made of real poop." —ANNE FRANK

"Men who consistently leave the toilet seat up secretly want women to get up to go to the bathroom in the middle of the night and fall in." —RITA RUDNER

> Knock-knock!
>
> Who's there?
>
> Figs.
>
> Figs who?
>
> Figs the toilet! You clogged it.

 What did one fireman say to the other in the bathroom?

Fire in the hole!

What did the boss hang up in the bathroom for the employees to read?

A list of doo-doos and don'ts.

Knock-knock!

Who's there?

Howard.

Howard who?

Howard you like to turn on a fan after what you just did to the bathroom?

What did Rudolph say to Santa when his bathroom break lasted too long?

Can you wrap it up in there?

Knock-knock!

Who's there?

Watt.

Watt who?

Watt died in here?

Knock-knock!

Who's there?

Ooze.

Ooze who?

Ooze gonna clean up this toilet?

**Did you hear about Paul,
the greatest plumber in the world?**

Don't talk to him. He's pooped.

Knock-knock!

Who's there?

Diploma.

Diploma who?

Diploma is here to fix the toilet.

Why did the chicken cross the road?

To get to the bathroom.

Did you hear about the sheep that went to the bathroom together?

They were tightly knit.

Knock-knock!

Who's there?

Butter.

Butter who?

Butter not tell you what I just did in the bathroom.

**How do you know
it's time to go to the bathroom?**

When the coffee cup's empty.

**What should a plumber
never bring to a potluck?**

Beef stew.

**What do you call someone
who spends more than half an hour
in the bathroom each morning?**

Dad.

**What did the toilet bowl say when
Patrick took a seat?**

"Make way! He's gonna blow!"

**Why did the barber use the alley
on the way to the bathroom?**

He liked making
short cuts.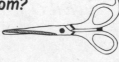

Real Movies

Real movies that sound like something you would do in the bathroom:

- *Hot Fuzz*
- *Blown Away*
- *Forces of Nature*
- *The Remains of the Day*
- *Children of the Corn*
- *Gone with the Wind*
- *The Blob*
- *Dirty Work*
- *Something's Gotta Give*

What's the worst thing someone can do in the bathroom?

Mistake the toilet brush for a toothbrush.

Knock-knock

Who's there?

Sausage.

Sausage who?

Sausage a mess you left in that bathroom.

What did the cowboy have to say about his trip to the bathroom?

It was an okie dookie.

Why did the boy fill the bathtub with mice?

He wanted to be squeaky clean.

What are relief maps for?

Finding the bathroom.

**What's the grossest device
to listen to music with?**

An iPood.

**What is a plumber's
favorite amusement park ride?**

The log flume.

**When you use a toilet on the airplane,
where does the poop go?**

Nowhere—they never clean those toilets.

**What do you use
to unlock the bathroom door?**

A doo-key.

JOHN: What is purple, has spikes, and can sing a beautiful tune?

LOU: I don't know. What?

JOHN: A dookie.

LOU: What? A dookie is none of those things!

JOHN: I know. I just wanted to make the riddle difficult to solve.

STUDENT: Teacher, can I go to the bathroom?

TEACHER: No, no. May I go to the bathroom?

STUDENT: Hey, I asked first!

What is white, yellow, smooth, and deadly?
A shark-infested toilet.

What does the Pope do in the bathroom?
Holy crap.

What did the cannibal do after he dumped his girlfriend?
He wiped.

What kind of jokes do vampires like best?
Bat-room humor.

How can you find the bathroom in France?
Check with the *mon-sewer.*

Not the Best, but a Solid #2

TOILET TOMFOOLERY

What bathroom item is the biggest rip-off?

Toilet paper.

What did one toilet say to the other toilet?

Nothing—its mouth was full of water.

Knock-knock!

Who's there?

Donna.

Donna who?

Donna forget to flush when you're done in there!

What's the worst part about using an office bathroom?

The paperwork.

What is the stinkiest plant in the garden?

Toilet-trees.

What's on a roll every day?
Toilet paper!

**Did you hear about
the constipated mathematician?**
He worked it out with a pencil.

What kind of pencil did he use?
A #2 pencil.

Where do flies sit down to dinner?
On stools.

**Where should you never step
on a baseball diamond?**
Turd base.

**What did the serial killer
do to the toilet?**
He murdered it.

You Stink!

*Clever ways
to tell someone
that they
REALLY
need to take a shower.*

- You smell worse than a city dump full of dog poop.

- You smell like you ate a big bowl of farts for lunch.

- You smell like you forgot to take off every diaper you wore when you were a baby.

- You smell like you forgot to throw away the toilet paper when you were done with it.

- You smell like you took a dump instead of leaving it behind.

What do you call
a man who flushes the toilet?

So-flush-sticated.

> *Knock-knock!*
>
> *Who's there?*
>
> *Bernie.*
>
> *Bernie who?*
>
> *Bernie candle—
> it stinks in here!*

What's the biggest toilet
in the world?

The Super Bowl.

Why didn't Robin Hood
need a toilet?

He had his very own
Little John
always by his side.

What is a constipated gambler's favorite game?

Craps.

- -

Knock-knock!

Who's there?

Norma Lee.

Norma Lee who?

Norma Lee I don't leave
such a stink in the bathroom.

Apologies.

- -

What is a dump truck driver's lucky number?

Two.

- -

What's another name for the world's biggest toilet?

A swimming pool.

**Why didn't the baseball player
have any friends?**

Because he always had the runs.

**What did the comedian
say when he looked at his poop?**

Yuk, yuk.

Knock-knock!

Who's there?

Anita.

Anita who?

Anita go to the bathroom, now!

**Why can't cats nap
at the beach?**

Because they don't sleep
in their litter box.

> Knock-knock!
>
> Who's there?
>
> Honey.
>
> Honey who?
>
> Honey, would you please flush the toilet
> when you're done in there?

Did you hear about the movie Constipation?
It was never released.

**What's the grossest cookbook
ever published?**
Dump Dinners.

Knock-knock!

Who's there?

Hyper.

Hyper who?

Hyper fur to use the bathroom at home.

Knock-knock!

Who's there?

Sherwood.

Sherwood who?

Sherwood be nice if you'd
bring me something to read because
I'm going to be in here awhile.

What do you call the guy who has to clean up after the animals?

A pookeeper.

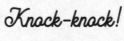

Knock-knock!

Who's there?

Justin.

Justin who?

Justin time to make it to the bathroom, whew!

You stink!

You Stink!

*More clever ways
to tell someone
that they
REALLY
need to take a shower.*

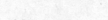

- A gas station bathroom would think you smell bad.

- You smell like a cat confused you with its litter box.

- You make natural gas seem like anything but natural.

- You smell like a fart and a poop had a race to see who could get out first, and they tied.

- Did you burp out of your butt and fart out of your mouth at the same time?

**Why do police officers
sit down when
they go to the bathroom?**

It's the best way to do their duty.

**What's the worst thing you can
do in the laundry room?**

Mistake the dryer for a toilet.

**Why did Beethoven go to the
bathroom in the woods?**

Because he wanted his poop
to decompose.

Knock-knock!

Who's there?

Harry.

Harry who?

Harry up, I need to get to the toilet!

Knock-knock!
Who's there?
Dwayne.
Dwayne who?
Dwayne the tub;
I need to use the toilet!

What did the toilet order at McDonalds?
A #2.

**Why didn't the monster
flush the toilet?**
He didn't need to.
He scared the crap out of it.

**What do you call someone
using an army latrine?**
A pooper trooper.

Knock-knock!

Who's there?

Dismay.

Dismay who?

*Dismay be the last time
I'll let you use my toilet.*

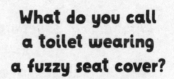

What do you call a toilet wearing a fuzzy seat cover?

A costume potty.

A little boy in church needed to go to the bathroom. "Mom, can I go take a dump?" he asked. "Yes," his mother replied, "but we're in church. Next time, don't say 'dump,' say 'whisper.' It's more polite." The next Sunday, the boy is sitting by his father, and again he needed to use the bathroom. "Dad, I have to whisper," the boy said. "Okay," the father replied. "Whisper in my ear."

Why wouldn't the baseball player use public toilets?

Because he liked home runs.

What happens after you eat too much alphabet soup?

You get really bad vowel movements.

> *Knock-knock!*
>
> *Who's there?*
>
> *Manuel.*
>
> *Manuel who?*
>
> *Manuel be sorry if you don't start flushing the toilet!*

Why do toilets love jokes so much?

Because they are always down in the dumps.

Knock-knock!

Who's there?

Bean.

Bean who?

Bean forgetting to put the seat down, haven't you?

What do you get after eating too much ice cream?

A chocolate swirl.

Knock-knock!

Who's there?

A pileup.

A pileup who?

A pileup poo in the toilet? You better flush!

What stinks and flies through the air at 500 mph?

An airplane bathroom.

What's brown, jumps, and lives in Australia?

The kangapoo.

Knock-knock!
Who's there?
Megan.
Megan who?
Megan logs in the toilet!

Knock-knock!

Who's there?

Russian.

Russian who?

Russian to the bathroom!

What's the crappiest candy?
Reese's feces.

**What's worse than finding
a fly in your soup?**
Finding a fly in your poop.

What's the difference between a clock and a toilet?

One is a time machine,
the other is a grime machine.

Knock-knock!

Who's there?

Maggot.

Maggot who?

Maggot snappy in there!
I gotta go number two!

What do you call a bathroom in Finland?

Helstinki.

How did the toilet paper hit the jackpot in a game of slots?

It was on a roll.

Knock-knock!

Who's there?

Hewlett.

Hewlett who?

Hewlett the seat up?

What does an umpire say after he takes a poop?

"You're out!"

What do you never appreciate until it's gone?

Toilet paper.

I am something in your bathroom.

I am found on a roll.

Every time I'm used,

I get dropped into a bowl.

What am I?

Toilet paper.

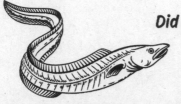

Did you hear about the girl who found electric eels in her toilet?

It was a shocking discovery!

Did you hear about the high-school kid who pooped out a misshapen log in total silence?

It was a Teenage Mutant Ninja Turdle.

Why did the secretary stay in the bathroom for so long?

Because no job is finished until the paperwork is done.

What do you call someone who is obsessed with toilet jokes?

A commodian.

Why did the dad only change his baby's diaper one time?

The box said "up to 20 pounds."

What do you do when you find blue poop in the toilet?

Try to cheer it up.

Where is the most painful place to go number two on a car trip?

A fork in the road.

Why do fish record how much they pooped?

They always have scales.

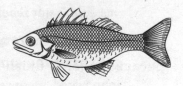

What's the easiest way to lose two pounds?

Drop off a deuce in the bathroom.

What animal is best at wiping itself clean?

An octopus, because it has so many arms.

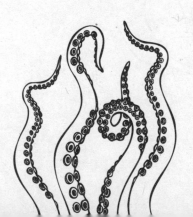

JOHN SWIFTIES

"I'm having some pretty bad diarrhea today,"
John gushed.

"Why is my voice so raspy?"
John asked phlegmatically.

"I couldn't hold it in any longer!"
John leaked.

"Honestly, it makes me want to vomit,"
was John's gut reaction.

"Don't you have anything to get rid of the smell in here?"
John asked, incensed.

> *Knock-knock!*
>
> *Who's there?*
>
> *Kent.*
>
> *Kent who?*
>
> *Kent you see this bathroom is occupied?*

Did you hear about the guy who posted online every time he pooped?

He had a log blog.

Why did the salesman poop in the furniture store?

Because the customer asked to see a stool sample.

What is cool, white, and has a bottom at the top?

A toilet.

What happens if you eat too many Mexican jumping beans?

Your poop will jump right out of the toilet.

*Did you hear about the guy who
got lost in the bathroom?*

He took a wrong turd.

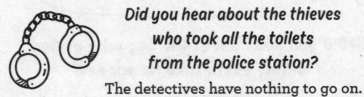

*Did you hear about the thieves
who took all the toilets
from the police station?*

The detectives have nothing to go on.

---

*I hold clean water like a glass
but you wouldn't want to drink from me.
What am I?*

A toilet.

---

*I'm a bowl but you wouldn't want to
eat cereal out of me. What am I?*

A toilet.

JOHN SWIFTIES

"I didn't make it to the bathroom in time,"
John burst out.

"I shouldn't have waited so long to clean the toilet,"
John said crustily.

"I pooped so hard I think my colon fell out!"
John said, feeling disorganized.

"I have flow issues,"
John sputtered.

"Better get some air circulating in here fast—it stinks!"
John said fanatically.

"The bulb burst in the bathroom, and I couldn't see what I was doing,"
John said delightedly.

What did the toilet say on Wheel of Fortune?

I'd like to buy a bowel, please!

What's the difference between a toilet brush and biscotti?

You can't dip a toilet brush in your coffee.

BILL: Did you have corn for lunch?

JOHN: Yes, how did you know?

BILL: You forgot to flush the toilet.

Why did the man like his toilet paper so much?

Because it was Charmin'.

Knock-knock!

Who's there?

Esther.

Esther who?

Esther any more toilet paper?

How is a scientist like a fly?

They both investigate stools.

A bear and a rabbit are pooping in the woods. The bear asked the rabbit, "Do you have problems with poop sticking to your fur?" The rabbit, a little confused, replied, "No." "That's great!" said the bear, as he grabbed the rabbit and started wiping.

Knock-knock!

Who's there?

Who.

Who who?

Who flushed that poor owl down the toilet?
I can hear it from here!

Where do pigs do their business?

In a pork-a-potty.

JOHN SWIFTIES

"Why is my voice so raspy?"
John asked phlegmatically.

**"I finished cleaning out the
septic tank,"**
John said emptily.

"These jokes make me wanna barf,"
John said wretchedly.

"While this over here is a toilet seat,"
John went on.

"I installed the new toilet!"
John said, flushed with success.

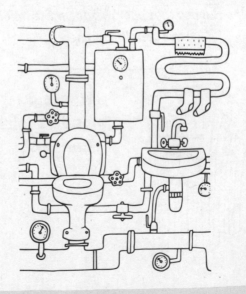

**How many logs
can you fit in an empty toilet?**

One.
After that, it isn't empty anymore.

Did you hear about this book?

It's a #2 best-seller!

**What did the roll of toilet paper
say to the toilet?**

Nothing. Toilet paper doesn't talk!

**What do dogs call
fire hydrants?**

Public toilets.

**What do you call an elephant
in a toilet bowl?**

Stuck.

What's the only TV show you can watch in the bathroom?

Game of Thrones.

Toilets really like it when you're polite,
so make sure to say your
pees and thank-poos.

What does a dog call a litter box?

An all-you-can-eat buffet.

Where does a baseball player rub toilet paper?

On his bat.

What did the one fly say to the other fly?

Excuse me,
is this stool taken?

Did you hear the joke about the toilet?

It's pretty filthy!

What's a toilet's favorite kind of frozen yogurt?

Chocolate.

What do dogs call firemen?

Toilet repairmen.

What do cows read when they're in the bathroom?

Cattle-logs.

What did the surfer say in the bathroom?

Wipe out!

Silent but Deadly

GASTASTIC QUIPS

What does a liar say?

"I didn't fart; it was the seat
that made the noise!"

What's worse than smelling a fart?

Tasting one.

**What's the difference
between a museum
and a chili cook-off?**

One is artsy, and the other is fartsy.

Knock-knock!

Who's there?

Pooh.

Pooh who?

**Pooh-lease stop farting
in the kitchen!**

Did you hear about the guy who desperately stumbled into the bathroom in the middle of the night and couldn't find the toilet?

It was a shart in the dark.

Who is the smelliest Ninja Turtle?

Leo-farto.

What is the grossest reality show?

Shart Tank.

How was the boy able to fart so loudly that it fell on a thousand ears?

He did it in a cornfield.

What's the most unpopular activity at summer camp?

Farts and Crafts.

Where does the government keep all the most valuable farts?

Fart Knox.

A fart is like a speech— it's not what you say, it's how you say it.

Why are farts worse than bad breath?

Because you can at least put a mint in your mouth.

What do you call it when you fart glitter?

Very interesting.

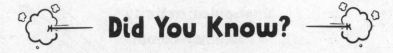

Did You Know?

- A fart is just a secret your butt whispers to your underwear.

- A shooting star is just another name for a farting comet.

- True happiness is getting to use your own toilet again after being away on vacation.

- Farting is like letting the wind out of your own sails.

- Farting is like letting go of a bad memory—if it stays with you, it'll poison you.

- Farting is like eating super-spicy hot wings—do it, and before you know it, way worse things are coming.

- Farting is playing a high-stakes game of Chicken with a poop.

**What would be the worst insect
to be reincarnated as?**
A stinkbug.

What did the crap say to the fart?
You blow me away.

**What do you call a pixie
who needs a bath?**
Stinker Belle.

Knock-knock!

Who's there?

Oliver.

Oliver who?

Oliver underwear stinks!

**What do you call
a guy who makes
armpit farts all night?**
A pit orchestra musician.

What drink will always make you burp?

Belch's Grape Juice.

What do you get when you cross a skunk with bells?

Jingle smells.

Knock-knock!

Who's there?

Interrupting fart.

Interrupting fart–

make fart noise

What's the smelliest retail store?

Walfart.

What do you call a stinky postman?

Mail-odious.

**What's yellow, has spiked hair,
and smells awful?**

Fart Simpson.

**What do you get after
you eat hamburgers?**

Ham-burp-gers.

**What do you call
passing gas in a pair
of borrowed pants?**

A fart transplant.

**Why do teenagers
fart so much?**

Because it is the only gas
they can afford.

**What do you call a person
that is too shy to fart in public?**

A private tooter.

What is the stinkiest country?

Fartgentina.

Knock-knock!

Who's there?

Candy.

Candy who?

Candy farting please stop now?

**How can you tell if
a person has a good imagination?**

They think their farts smell good.

**What do ninjas and some farts
have in common?**

They are both
silent and deadly.

Knock-knock!

Who's there?

Aida.

Aida who?

*Aida whole can of beans and
I'm ready to empty the gas tank.*

Knock-knock!

Who's there?

Boo.

Boo who?

Why are you crying? It was only a fart.

**What do a bowl of chili and
a filling station have in common?**

They both give you gas.

Where's the best place to buy beans?

At the
gas station.

Did you hear about the prince who ate too many beans?

It resulted in
noble gas.

Where do ghost farts come from?

Boooooooties.

Did you hear about the girl that was in love with the smell of her own farts?

She was inflatulated.

TYPES OF FARTS

*Farts come in
all shapes and sizes.
Have you ever experienced
any of these?*

- **The Crescendo:** A fart that starts quiet but just keeps getting LOUDER.

- **The Déjà Vu:** When you swear you've smelled something just like it before, somewhere, sometime.

- **The Trapper Keeper:** The hostile act of a fart in an enclosed space, like a compact car or an elevator.

- **The Zombie:** When a fart smells so nasty that you're sure you're dead and are slowly rotting from the inside out.

- **The Flamingo:** A fart so substantial that you have to stand on one leg to help it get out.

Knock-knock!
Who's there?
Rhino.
Rhino who?
Rhino you're the one who farted.

If you're an odious gas, life begins at farty.

What's the difference between the Mona Lisa and passing gas?

One is a work of art.
One is a work of fart.

Did you hear about the couple that were perfect for each other?

She was a heartbreaker and he was a fart-breaker.

**How can a fart
surprise you?**

If it's got a lump in it.

**What do you call
a group of superheroes
after a chili competition?**

The Fartastic Four.

Why does a black hole never fart?

Because nothing
can escape it!

Why did the skeleton belch?

It didn't have
the guts to fart.

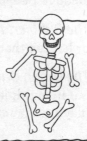

**What can go right through
your pants and not leave a hole?**

A fart.

TYPES OF FARTS

Farts come in all shapes and sizes. Have you ever experienced any of these?

- **The Rapid Fire:** A bunch of farts all at once that make a rat-tat-tat-tat-tat sound, like you're a machine gunner on a warship.

- **The Odorless Wonder:** A fart that's all noise and no smell but is still just as embarrassing.

- **Flavor Country:** A fart so nasty that you don't just smell it, but you taste it a little too.

- **The Bubbler:** A fart sneakily emitted in a bathtub or hot tub that just looks like a bigger bubble.

- **The Organ Grinder:** That rare fart that comes out in multiple tones so that it sounds like you're playing a jaunty, old-timey tune.

Where do farts go skating?

At the roller stink.

What do you call a fart you make in the laundry room?

A fluffy.

Knock-knock!

Who's there?

Wet.

Wet who?

Wet smells so bad?

Did you hear about the guy who ate an entire bowl of baked beans before going to the ballet?

He shouldn't have.

What do you call a baby's fart?

Little stinker.

---

*Did you hear about the grandma
who ate too much broccoli?*

She was an old fart.

---

*How many teenagers does it
take to stink up a room?*

Only a pew.

---

*Did you hear about the incident
at the bean factory?*

There was a gas leak.

---

*Did you hear about
the fart factory that not only
made farts but also sold them?*

Their motto was,
"Whoever smelt it, dealt it."

How does a cow's fart smell?
Udderly terrible.

Knock-knock!

Who's there?

Hoof.

Hoof who?

Hoof farted?

What cat loves beans the most?
Puss in Toots.

What did the brave man do?
Took a chance on a fart
after a day of diarrhea.

**What do you call a dinosaur
that farts too much?**
Stinky-saurus.

A FART IS JUST A POOP

- that doesn't believe in itself.
- that's calling to let you know it's running late.
- that hasn't reached its potential.
- that isn't thinking hard enough.
- that's sounding the evacuation alarm.
- that's honking for your butthole to get out of the way.

What did the astronaut say before he farted?

Blast off!

What's the stinkiest piece of clothing?

A windbreaker.

Did you hear about the boy who couldn't stop farting in class?

He was a-gassed!

What do you call a Mozart fart?

Classical gas.

What university smells the worst?

P.U.

What smells worse?
A burp or a fart?

Hard to say, but together
they could knock out a horse.

What are grizzly bear farts like?
Silent but violent.

What can clear a room
faster than a fart?

An angry skunk.

What did the skunk say
to the farting man?

"No need to make such a stink,
I've got you covered."

DID YOU KNOW?

- Farting is the original air mail.

- Farting is just your body making thunder before the lightning.

- Farting is just your butt being jealous of your talking, singing mouth.

- Farting is a literal example of somebody butting into the conversation.

- Pooping is just having one last goodbye with a meal you truly loved.

- A poop is just a fart that worked hard and applied itself.

- Farting while you're eating is just a "coming attraction."

COMING SOON

Why shouldn't you fart in an Apple store?

They don't have
Windows.

Why won't vampires feast on meteorologists?

They give them wind.

Knock-knock!

Who's there?

Gas.

Gas who?

Gas who stunk up the bathroom?

Why was the surfer scared to go into the water?

Sharts were circling.

Why did Pocahontas eat a bag of jellybeans and then fart?

Because she wanted to paint with all the colors of the wind.

Why was the RV so stinky?

Because it was full of gas.

I didn't fart. That was just my bowels blowing you a kiss!

Why can you only put 239 beans in a can?

Because one more would make it "too farty."

TOP FIVE BEST PLACES TO FART:

1. Walking past first-class while boarding a plane.

2. In the library next to the rude person who is being too loud.

3. In an elevator if you're riding with someone who didn't return a hello.

4. When someone cuts in line behind you.

5. In your coach's office, after you've just been cut from the team.

How do you make a pig fly?
Feed it a bowl of beans.

What's the gassiest fish in the ocean?
The pufferfish.

**What do you call a monkey
that farts in church?**
A badboon.

**Want to know an easy way to
transform your tub into a Jacuzzi?**
Take a bath after eating
broccoli casserole.

Knock-knock!

Who's there?

Omar.

Omar who?

*Omar goodness, these farts
are horrible!*

What's invisible and smells like bananas?

Monkey farts.

Did you hear about the lost fart?

He turned into a burp.

Why did the teenager finally quit farting?

He ran out of gas.

What is the stinkiest day of the week?

Tootsday.

What is rude, can travel through solid material, and can bring you to tears?

Farts.

Did you hear about the T-rex that didn't have the ability to fart?

It faced ex-stink-tion.

Did you hear about the turkey with a flatulence problem?

It shot stuffing all the way across the Thanksgiving table.

Did you hear about the fart that went on an adventure?

It made a great escape!

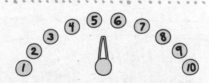

Why did the woman pass gas in the elevator?

She wanted to take her farts to a new level.

Why did the boy fart in the cemetery?

Because he read a tombstone that said RIP.

Did you hear about the fart joke book?

It was a best smeller!

Did you hear about the kid who just turned ten and ate too much prune cake?

He turned his birthday party into a birthday farty.

Knock-knock!

Who's there?

Mya.

Mya who?

Mya stomach's killing me from all these beans.

TYPES OF FARTS

Farts come in all shapes and sizes. Have you ever experienced any of these?

- **The Whodunit:** A silent but stinky fart in a crowded place. Only you know who was responsible. (It was you!)

- **The Drowned Out:** A fart let loose in a place so loud—a concert, a sporting event, a dance club—that nobody knows you did it.

- **The Forgiven:** A fart in church that nobody is going to call you out for.

- **The Fair Warning:** It may feel, sound, and smell like a simple fart, but you understand it for what it is: a two-minute warning to get to the bathroom—fast.

- **The Mosquito Bite:** A fart that hurts just a little bit.

What is the stinkiest dog?

The Poo-dle.

What do you get
when you fart
in a shepherd's pie?

Never invited over for dinner again.

What smells like
ham and filth?

Pig farts.

What happens when you cross
an atomic bomb
with beans?

A weapon of gas destruction!

What kind of pizza
smells like farts?

Poop-eroni.

Have you heard about the new line of fartphones?

I wouldn't buy one.
They're real stinkers.

Did you hear about the bad student with bad gas?

He kept getting farter behind,
so his parents hired him a tooter.

How do you make still water turn to sparkling?

Easy, just fart
in the glass!

Why can't farts get a decent education?

Because they always get expelled.

JOHN: What's the best way to catch a fart?

LOU: Why would anyone want to catch a fart?

LITTLE JOHNNY: Mom! Dad! I was the only kid who knew the answer to the question the teacher asked today!

MOM: That's wonderful! What was the question?

LITTLE JOHNNY: Who farted?

MIKE: I farted at work, and my coworkers had to open a window.

SARAH: Must have been really bad—you're flight attendants.

How did the ninja hide his fart?

He masked it.

Why do horses fart when they gallop?

They wouldn't achieve full horsepower if they didn't.

What did the circus monkey say when the clown farted?

Nothing. It smelled so funny that he couldn't stop laughing long enough to say anything!

Knock-knock!

Who's there?

Pencil.

Pencil who?

Pencil be stained if you keep making those juicy farts!

What causes
cold winter winds?

Frosty the Snowman,
after eating a bowl of chili.

Knock-knock!

Who's there?

Pea.

Pea who?

Pea-yew! What did you eat?

Why are farts
so wholesome?

Because it's what's on the inside
that counts.

What do you call a scientist
who studies elemental gases?

A fartologist.

What do you call it when a ghost farts?

A spirited toot.

Why did the gassy chicken cross the road?

To get to the odor side.

Why did the turkey need a bath?

It smelled fowl.

In space, no one can hear you fart. And if you're wearing a spacesuit, only you can smell it.

**How does a burp cut loose
and get a little crazy?**

It goes out the other end.

**What's invisible and smells
like carrots and cabbage?**

Rabbit farts.

**What did one burp
say to the other?**

Let's be stinkers and go backwards.

**Why didn't the pig laugh
at the loud fart?**

Because he was being
a real boar.

What's the stinkiest city?

Pitts-burgh.

**What's green
and smells like flies?**

Kermit's farts.

**Why did the conductor
fart so loud?**

He wanted to toot his own horn.

Why do farts smell so bad?

So your deaf Grandpa
can enjoy them too!

**How do you keep a skunk
from smelling?**

Hold its nose.

Hot Messes

SLOPPY GAGS

What do you have after you eat a prune pizza?

Pizzeria!

**What do you call
a comedian with
irritable bowel syndrome?**

The life of the potty.

**What day of the week
should you never use a public restroom?**

Splatterday.

Knock-knock!

Who's there?

Peas.

Peas who?

Peas pass the soap;
I got something on my finger.

Did you hear about the diarrhea outbreak?

You should have. It's all over town.

Knock-knock!
Who's there?
My.
My who?
My tissues can't clean this mess up!

What's the most disgusting kids' book ever written?
Diarrhea of a Wimpy Kid.

What do you call a kid with a bad case of the runs?
Down in the dumps.

What do you give an elephant with diarrhea?
Room.

Why won't vampires feast on joggers?
They give them the runs.

**What basketball team
can't control their bowels?**
The San Antonio Spurts.

**What do you call a telephone worker
who took too many laxatives?**
A smooth operator.

**What's the one thing in the world
that feels even better
than being in love?**
Finding a clean toilet
when you're out in public
and diarrhea strikes.

Knock-knock!

Who's there?

Albee.

Albee who?

Albee throwing up if
I eat any more hot dogs!

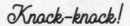

Knock-knock!

Who's there?

Alda.

Alda who?

Alda potato salad got spoiled.
The bathroom will be toxic!

What does the lifeguard say after he goes to the bathroom?

"Everybody
out of the pool!"

An Age-Old Problem

A 60-year-old, a 70-year-old, and an 80-year-old were all playing bingo when the 60-year-old said, "Being 60 is the worst age. I sit on the toilet all day and I can't pee at all!"

"That's nothing," said the 70-year-old. "I can't even poop!"

"No," said the 80-year-old. "I have the worst age."

"Do you have trouble peeing?" the 60-year-old asked.

"No, not at all. Every day at 6 a.m."

"What about pooping?" the 70-year-old asked.

"Not a problem. 6:30 a.m.," he said.

"So you're telling me," the 70-year-old said, "that you have the hardest age, but you can pee and poop easily? What's the problem?"

"The problem is that I don't get up till 8 o'clock."

**What do you call a supermodel with
a bad case of diarrhea?**

A hot mess.

What happens after you eat peppers?
They get jalapeño dirty business.

**Did you hear about
the basketball player who had diarrhea?**

He got called out
for double-dribbling.

**Did you hear about the new album
by the band Diarrhea?**

It leaked early.

**Did you hear about the man who didn't poop
for months and then got diarrhea?**
Talk about a blast from the past.

> Knock-knock!
>
> Who's there?
>
> Esther.
>
> Esther who?
>
> Esther a doctor on call?
> My diarrhea is out of control!

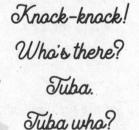

What drink is both disgusting and refreshing?
Cherry Slimeade.

What's the stickiest kind of jazz music?
Scat.

Knock-knock!

Who's there?

Tuba.

Tuba who?

Tuba toothpaste stuck to the sink.

Knock-knock!
Who's there?
Jamaica.
Jamaica who?
Jamaica mess in this bathroom?

**What do you get
when you eat a candy bar,
throw it up, take it to a
cabin in the woods,
and then eat
the candy bar again?**

A retreat.

Knock-knock!

Who's there?

Will.

Will who?

Will you get me the air freshener?
It stinks in here!

What did the chef say to the toilet?

One dinner,
coming right up!

What's the best way to avoid getting sick in the car?

Roll down the window.

Why did the girl get sick at the haunted house?

It was too spew-key.

How did the bucket know he was about to vomit?

He was looking a little pail.

*Did you hear about the jogger
looking for the bathroom?*

He had the runs.

---

*What is grosser than a number two after lunch
at an all-you-can-eat Indian buffet?*

Not much.

What's the grossest-tasting bean?

Dung beans.

*What flavor of ice cream
will make you sick?*

Van-ill-a.

---

*What special treat do you get
the night of St. Patrick's Day?*

A bowlful of Irish spew.

Knock-knock!

Who's there?

Hatch.

Hatch who?

Ewww, don't sneeze in my face!

Did you hear about the cow with diarrhea?

It was an udder disaster!

Knock-knock!

Who's there?

Stan.

Stan who?

Stan back.
I'm about to spew!

Why do they call it a litter of puppies?

Because they mess up
the whole house.

Knock-knock!

Who's there?

Hugh.

Hugh who?

Hugh pooped all over the bathroom and forgot to clean it up?

What's the difference between puke and school lunch?

School lunch comes on a plate.

What's the worst way to get your feet dirty?

When you mix up your thong underwear with your thong sandals.

Who shouts "tee-hee" when you poke him in the stomach and then makes a huge mess?

Poopin' Fresh.

What's another name for monster barf?

Ghoul-ash.

Why did eating the chair with the broken leg make me vomit?

Because it didn't sit well.

Knock-knock!

Who's there?

Carrie.

Carrie who?

Carrie me to a toilet—
I'm gonna spew!

What did the lady with a run in her stockings do?

She got to a bathroom, quick!

FUNNY PUKE NAMES

- Liquidation sale
- Spew
- Tossing cookies
- Lunch summons
- Retching
- Making stew
- Feeding Poseidon
- Porcelain offering
- Upchuck
- Pit stop at regurgitation station
- Hurling
- Liquid moan

Why did the zombie take a sick day?
He was feeling rotten.

What do dogs call vomit?
Second dinner.

**What's red, chunky, and
smells like a gazelle?**
Cheetah puke.

**Which monster will make
the biggest mess out of your bathroom?**
The Loch Mess Monster.

**Why did the Loch Ness Monster
eat the ship?**
He was craving
Cap'n Crunch.

What should you do if pigs start to fly?

Get an umbrella.

Two bats were hanging in their cave. The first bat asked the second, "Do you remember the worst day of your life?" The second bat replied, "Yeah. The day I had diarrhea!"

Why did the bear throw up after eating George Washington?

Because it is hard to keep a good man down.

What's green, slimy, and smells like peanuts?

Elephant puke.

What is the most nauseating city?

Barf-celona.

Why did the criminal enjoy vomiting?

Because it's ill-egal.

Knock-knock!

Who's there?

Butternut.

Butternut who?

Butternut step in that steaming pile over there.

What do you name a dog that throws up all the time?

Ralph.

*I just can't help telling
jokes about vomiting.
What can I say?
It's a sickness!*

**How can you tell the difference
between a healthy dog
and a sick dog?**

 One barks, the other barfs.

**What beats throwing up out of
a speeding car window?**

Your heart.

**Where is the most
entertaining place to puke?**

A hot-air balloon.
(Not so entertaining
for anyone else, though.)

*Did you hear about the girl that puked
up her lunch into the bowl?*

No? I'll spare you.

---

*Have a friend celebrating a barfday? Help them
get into the party mood by singing this song!*

Happy barf day to you,
You sat in my spew,
Now you smell like vomit,
Happy barf day to you!

What's worse than eating vomit soup?

Eating day-old vomit soup.

---

*What airline
does everyone get sick on?*

Spew-nited.

MOTION
SICKNESS
BAG

What do Italians call vomiting?

Barf-a-roni.

What happened to the teenager who drank eight sodas?

He threw 7 Up.

What's soft and warm at bedtime but hard and stiff in the morning?

Vomit.

Did you hear about the guy who missed the puke bucket and vomited all over the floor?

It was beyond the pail!

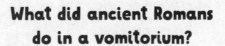

What did ancient Romans do in a vomitorium?

Un-wine.

FUNNY PUKE NAMES

- Making monster food
- Visiting the ejection seat
- Blowing chunks
- Yelling for Ralph
- The ol' heave ho
- The technicolor yawn
- Hugging the toilet
- Hit the eject button
- Blowing beans
- Horking
- The urp burp
- Chunder
- Chili storm

*Did you hear about
the professional golfer
who was so nervous about
the tournament that he threw up?*
Suppose it's just barf
for the course.

Do you want to hear a joke about vomit?
Coming right up!

*What machine plays music so bad
it makes you want to vomit?*
A pukebox.

Knock-knock!
Who's there?
Maura.
Maura who?
*Maura that spoiled macaroni salad, and
you'll never leave the bathroom again.*

Why did the baker have smelly hands?

"Because he kneaded a poop!"

*Did you hear about
the lion with diarrhea?*

It was a cat-astrophe.

Two girls were walking in the woods. They came across a pile of dog poop. "Is that dog poop?" the first girl asked. "Smells like dog poop," said the other. Then they both put their finger in it. "Feels like dog poop." Then they both put their fingers in their mouths and said, "Tastes like dog poop. Good thing we didn't step in it!"

*Did you hear about
the guy who vomited
while skydiving?*

It was all over town.

How did the T-Rex feel after vomiting all night?

Dino-sore.

What do you say to someone who's been throwing up all day long?

Happy barf-day!

Did you hear about the pilot who barfed on the plane?

He got through it with flying colors.

What happened when the kindergartener got sick during fingerprinting class?

She made a retch-a-sketch.

Why did the armadillo cross the road?

To show that he had guts.

Why did the ballerina get sick?

Because too much twirling
can make a girl hurl.

Did you hear about the man who couldn't stop pooping and vomiting at the same time?

It's a pretty sick joke.

What's small, cuddly, and green?

A koala that needs to puke.

What meal is sure to make you vomit?

Yak stew.

This is the last joke about vomiting.

I promise not
to bring that up anymore.

POLICE: Sir, please open the door and come out immediately.

MAN: But I'm pooping!

POLICE: Yes, but you're in a taxi.

BILL: How do you define messy?

JOHN: Dirty and unorganized?

BILL: No, the bathroom after you get done with it!

I vomited at the library today.

The librarian told me
to keep it down.

**What do you call
a vegan with diarrhea?**

A salad shooter.

**What do dogs
call their own vomit?**

The soup course.

**What animal
always throws up after it eats?**

A yak.

**When is laughter
the worst medicine?**

When you have diarrhea.

Pick Me a Winner

DIGGING FOR GOLD

What do boogers and nerds have in common?

People like to pick on them.

What's a nose's favorite movie?

Boogie Nights.

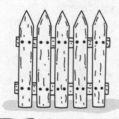

What do you call a wall of boogers?

A picket fence.

Did you hear about the booger who liked to gossip?

He was pretty nosy.

What's full of boogers and smells?

A nose.

TYPES OF SNOT

- **The Snail:** A long, slimy trail of snot.

- **Chunky Monkey:** When you have hard boogers stuck on top of slimy boogers.

- **The Broken Faucet:** When you've got a cold or allergies, and a bunch of snot just pours right out of your nose when you lean over.

- **The Old-Timer:** A booger that's so old and dry that it's gone from green to gray.

Why do we have fingernails?

So we can dig deeper!

What did the ear overhear
the other ear saying?

There's something between us that smells.

What does a booger
say to his girlfriend?

I'm stuck on you.

Where do boogers go
on vacation?

Snotland.

Did you hear
the nose got back together
with a bunch of snot?

It was an old phlegm.

**What do you say to your
snot-nosed friend when they're hungry?**

Go to Booger King.

**What do you get
if you put peppers
in your nose?**

A hot boogie.

**Why did the booger
and the pimple team up?**

They were sick of being picked on!

Knock-knock!

Who's there?

Bella.

Bella who?

Bella button's full of lint!

TYPES OF SNOT

- **The Nose Dandruff:** A dry, flaky booger that just falls out of your nose of its own volition.

- **The Clinger:** A booger that just won't come loose, no matter how hard you try.

- **Tenacious B:** A booger that you try to flick away, but it won't budge. Or, even worse, it moves over to the other finger you're using to flick it off.

- **The Fugitive:** A booger that you just can't seem to grab, and it gets farther and farther up there the more you try.

What button stinks most?

A belly button.

Why is there no such thing as an empty nose?

Because even a clean one
has fingerprints.

Did you hear about the guy who could pick his nose, dance, and play the trumpet all at the same time?

They called him the
Boogie Woogie Bugle Boy.

Why did the loogey die of old age?

Because slime flies!

Did you hear about the astronomer with saggy pants?

It was a half moon.

How are boogers and fruits similar?

Both get picked and eaten.

Did you hear about the guy whose nose ran for three months straight?

Snot funny.

Why did John hate his nose?

Because it didn't
smell very good.

Where can you find someone who's never picked their nose?

Nowhere.
That person has never existed.

What did the booger say when the magician asked for a volunteer?

Pick me! Pick me!

What do noses and apple pies have in common with each other?

They're both crusty.

> Knock-knock!
>
> Who's there?
>
> Boogie.
>
> Boogie who?
>
> Boogie hangin' from your nose!

What did the finger do when the nose went on strike?

Picket.

What monster can stick to walls?

The boogie-man.

What's thick, slimy, and hangs from tall trees?

Giraffe snot.

TYPES OF SNOT

- **The Phantom:** When you pick one and it just . . . disappears.

- **The Trophy:** A booger so big and that took you so long to get out that you kind of want to show it off to everybody.

- **The Mysterious Cave:** When you pick your nose because it's irritated and there aren't any boogers or snot in there at all.

- **Dracula's Delight:** Bloody boogers.

What's inside of a haunted spirit's nose?

Booo-gers.

What was the nose so melancholy about?

It didn't get picked.

What do you call a ball of snot wearing a motorcycle helmet?

A snail!

What's yellow, sticky, and smells like bananas?

Monkey snot.

What's a booger's favorite casino in Vegas?

The Golden Nugget.

What do noses and Brie cheese have in common?

They both smell and get runny.

What do you call the biggest booger in the world?

Green Giant.

What runs in most families?

Noses.

What did the kid say to the booger?

It's been nice gnawing you.

What do you call a Roman emperor with a cold?

Julius Sneezer.

Fancy Words for Boogers

*For when you need
to be dignified
about your bodily functions.*

- Nostril pickings
- Gold dust
- Hidden gems
- Upper crusts
- Boogeaux
- Nasal soil
- Nose noodles
- Crusty critters
- Nostril nuggets
- Buried treasure
- Little green men
- Chewy gooeys

*Why did the elephant
pick his nose?*

He wanted a quarter-pounder
for lunch.

Knock-knock!

Who's there?

Tom Sawyer.

Tom Sawyer who?

Tom Sawyer pickin' your nose.

*What did the booger's dad
say to his son when he talked back?*

Don't be snotty with me!

Who is the snottiest writer?

Ian Phlegming.

What's another name for a slug?

Look in your nose.

What is a gross kid's favorite food?

Ham-boogers.

What do you do if you see a hardworking booger?

Pick it!

Why was the nose so excited?

Because it was time to boogie woogie.

Knock-knock!
Who's there?
Throat.
Throat who?
Throat out that tissue.
It's full of boogers.

Knock-knock!

Who's there?

Snot.

Snot who?

Snot a good idea to pick your nose in church.

What's the difference between boogers and Brussels sprouts?

No one eats Brussels sprouts.

What did the diabetic woman find in her nose?

A sugar booger.

Why was the nose so sad?

Because it was always getting picked on.

What do you call a booger that's been on a diet?

Slim Pickins.

Ear wax monikers:

- Sticky icky
- Ear turds
- Headphone honey
- Witches' butter
- Ear snot
- Ear candy
- Super goo
- Ear jam
- Q-tip food
- Ear boogers
- Canal candle

**What's worse than
having an ear full of earwax?**
Having an ear full of earwigs.

 **Why did the little boy
only eat boogers?**
He was a picky eater.

A little boy picked his nose, then licked his finger. His father noticed him doing it and said, "Son, stop that! That is absolutely disgusting!" Then he took a tissue and wiped the booger off his finger. "Hey, I should be the one mad at you," the boy said. "And why is that?" his father asked. "I didn't get to flick it, and that's the most fun part!"

Knock-knock!

Who's there?

Otto.

Otto who?

Otto earwax, better eat
some belly button lint!

Urine
for a Treat

GOLDEN OLDIES

Why are people who pee a lot
so laid back?

Because they go with the flow.

Which Pokémon
can't control its bladder?

Squirtle.

What is the moon's
favorite song to sing
in the bathroom?

"Tinkle, Tinkle, Little Star."

Knock-knock!
Who's there?
Mage.
Mage who?
Mage ya laugh so hard
you peed yourself.

What's the difference between apple juice and pee?

A kid will wash their hands
if they get covered in apple juice.

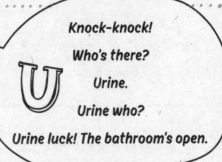

Knock-knock!

Who's there?

Urine.

Urine who?

Urine luck! The bathroom's open.

What do you get when you eat asparagus and cabbage?

The worst-smelling bathroom
of all time.

What do you get if you accidently dribble urine on the floor?

A mop!

Why did the pig pee all over his pen?

He wanted to go hog wild.

What did the cat say when the dog that was trying to pee?

Looks like you need a leg up!

Did you hear about the singer who drank too much soda before he got on his tour bus and wound up urinating in his pants?

Poor Justin Pee-ber.

What do you call it when a dinosaur urinates?

Pee-rex.

Why was the crocodile's pee so yellow?

He drank too much Gator-ade.

Knock-knock!

Who's there?

Ike.

Ike who?

Ike can't help but pee a little bit when I poop.

What did the computer programmer say before going to the bathroom?

Excuse me, I need to check my IP address.

What is the quickest way to become European?

Go to the bathroom.

What's a toilet's serial number?
4U2PN.

What's the best thing about swimming in the ocean?
Nobody will notice if you pee a little.

What's the worst thing to find in your freezer?
Frozen pees.

What's the worst-tasting cake in the world?
A urinal cake.

How do you know if you've embarrassed a toilet?
It flushes.

Why do men take showers instead of baths?

Because peeing in the bathtub is gross!

Why should you never eat a banana peel?

Because it's mostly pee.

How did the itsy-bitsy spider fall into the toilet bowl?

Down came the urine and washed the spider out.

Why did the star go to the bathroom?

It needed to tinkle.

I Gotta Take a Leak!

Oh, come on, you can do better than that. Here are a few alternatives.

- Checking my fluid levels
- Raising the water level
- Paying the water bill
- Paying the piper
- Recycling some beverages

What smells like asparagus but tastes way worse than asparagus?

Asparagus pee.

What did Elsa sing while she was on the toilet?

"Let it flow, let it flow . . ."

What did the mama say to the boy who peed on the rose bushes?

Urine trouble.

Every day at five o'clock, thousands of people rush home to use the toilet. It's flush hour!

**How do you wash your hands
in a urinal?**

Use the soap at the bottom.

**Does your grandpa have to wear
disposable underwear?**

Depends.

**What did the plumber
say to his apprentice?**

Urine for a surprise!

Which nut is always in the bathroom?

A pee-can.

**Why did the mummy not make it
to the bathroom in time?**

He took too long
to get unwrapped.

I Gotta Take a Leak!

*Oh, come on, you can
do better than that.
Here are a few alternatives.*

- Making an addition to the water table
- Putting out a fire
- Making it rain
- Shaking the dew off the flowers
- Checking to see if the plumbing is working correctly

**Did you hear
my new joke about pee?**

No.

Good, no one leaked it.

**What's the difference between
boiled eggs and pea soup?**

Anyone can boil eggs.

What do you call a dairy farmer's pee?

Cheese Whiz.

---

*A hike is just a walk
in nature's bathroom.*

**What is the most refreshing
thing to do when you pee?**

Crack open a soda poop.

Knock-knock!
Who's there?
European.
European who?
European on my shoes!

Have you ever heard of an ool?
It's a pool with no pee in it;
they're very rare!

**What's the wettest nation
on Earth?**
Urination.

**How does urine
get out of the body?**
It climbs a bladder.

What days of the week is your urine stream at its strongest?

Saturdays and Sundays.
All the others are just weak days.

How do you know you've had one too many sodas?

When your pee is fizzy.

Knock-knock!

Who's there?

Water.

Water who?

Water you doing in there?
Hurry up and pee!

What does the King of England call his toilet?

The Royal Throne.

Which of the Great Lakes has the most pee in it?

Lake Urine.

What does a baseball player say when he goes to the bathroom?

Bladder up.

Why didn't Shakespeare make it to the bathroom in time?

Because he couldn't decide whether to pee, or not to pee.

What do you call it when you urinate on a golf course?

A tee-pee.

BOY: Can I go to the bathroom?

TEACHER: Only if you can sing the alphabet.

BOY: ABCDEFGHIJKLMNOQRSTUVWXYZ

TEACHER: Where's the P?

BOY: Halfway down my leg!

What do you call a person who pees too much?

A whiz-ard.

Do you want to join the pee club?

Congratulations, urine!

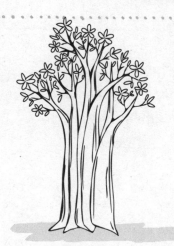

What did the man say after he peed in the forest?

"Tree whiz!"

What do they call urinals in Russia?

Yuri-nals.

What's the difference between a pineapple and a diaper?

One is full of Ps and one is full of pee.

How do you know you go to the bathroom too much?

You consider "10,000 Flushes" to be a challenge.

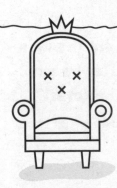

What do you call a really expensive chair that smells like pee?

A throne.

Why did the lawn go the bathroom?

Because it needed a sprinkle.

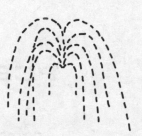

Knock-knock!

Who's there?

Don.

Don who?

Don think you can get away with peeing on the seat again!

How do you make sure you don't get a baby shower?

Be alert when you change his diaper.

PEE-EW

More Ways to Say Pee

- Sun showers
- Bitter lemonade
- Mountain Dew
- Mellow Yellow
- Recycled apple juice
- Emptying the bladder before there's a splatter
- Liquid sunshine
- Brine without the pickles

Which teacher made the biggest splash?

The PE teacher.

Where does Harry Potter go to the bathroom?

The headquarters at the Order of the Pee-nix.

Knock-knock!

Who's there?

Ice cream.

Ice cream who?

Ice cream if you don't put the seat down next time!

Why does a beach smell like urine?

Because the sea weed.

Doctors on the Runs

MEDICAL MISCHIEF

Why are constipated old men so rude?

Because they
don't give a crap.

**What did the food poisoning
do to the man's bowels?**

It rectum.

Knock-knock!

Who's there?

Noah.

Noah who?

Noah any good laxatives?

**What did the contest winner
with bad breath get?**

A plaque attack.

PATIENT: Doctor, you gotta help me. I think I've got hemorrhoids.

DOCTOR: Swell!

✚

PATIENT: Doctor, I've caught a bug.

DOCTOR: I apologize for that. I thought this hospital was pest free.

✚

PATIENT: Doctor, you gotta help me. I've got a massive pain in the rear.

DOCTOR: Really? I've always liked your husband.

✚

DOCTOR: We need your blood type, sir.

VAMPIRE: Any type will do!

✚

PATIENT: Doctor! I accidentally got a spoon stuck up there!

DOCTOR: Relax, don't make such a stir.

Why did the car with a dead battery and the constipated kid have in common?

Neither one could go.

Did you hear about the redhead whose breath stinks?

Her dentist said it was because she had ginger-vitis.

What's frozen, falls from the sky, and stinks?

Hail-itosis.

Do you want to hear a secret?

If it's that you have bad breath, that's no secret.

Where did the gross girl save her fingernails?

In a nail file.

Did you hear about the guy whose armpits were so smelly that they made his Speed Stick slow down and reconsider?

What do you call a knight with bad acne?

Sir Picks-a-Lot.

Knock-knock!

Who's there?

Termite.

Termite who?

Termites the night I can finally go poo, thanks to these laxatives!

**What's the nastiest habit
a proctologist can have?**
Nail-biting.

**Why did the kid
with food poisoning
have to stay at home?**
It was doctor's odors.

A doctor handed a patient a specimen cup
and said, "You can go fill this up in there,"
pointing to the bathroom. A few minutes
later, the patient came out and handed the
empty cup to the doctor. "I didn't need this.
There was a toilet in there, so I used that."

**Why did the bacon
go to the hospital?**
It wanted to be cured.

What is dandruff's favorite cereal?

Anything with flakes.

How can you tell if a book was written by a proctologist?

Lots and lots of colons.

Why did the banana go to the doctor?

It wasn't peeling well.

Why did the witch say she came to see the doctor?

"Hubble, bubble, urine trouble."

MAN: Doctor, you gotta help me! Every morning when I wake up and look in the mirror, I throw up. What's wrong with me?

DOCTOR: I'm not sure, but your eyesight is perfect.

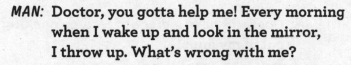

MAN: Doctor, I'm having trouble breathing.

DOCTOR: Don't worry, we will soon put a stop to that!

✚

DOCTOR: Ma'am, I'm afraid I have some bad news. You have a hard time paying attention, as well as severe diarrhea.

WOMAN: Oh dear! Well, at least I don't have severe diarrhea.

✚

PATIENT: Doctor, I need a medication for constipation.

DOCTOR: Here you are, sir. This is the #1 doctor-rated laxative on the market.

PATIENT: That's great, but I'd really prefer the #2.

MAN: Doctor! I have a piece of lettuce peeking out of my anus!

DOCTOR: That's troubling—it's just the tip of the iceberg.

✚

PATIENT: Doctor, doctor, you gotta help me!

DOCTOR: What seems to be the problem?

PATIENT: There's a big crack in my butt!

✚

PATIENT: Doctor, I threw my back out. Can you do anything for me?

DOCTOR: I can check the trash for you.

✚

PATIENT: Doctor, I keep making wind around my wife!

DOCTOR: Tell her to buy a kite.

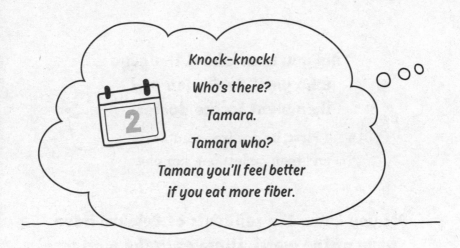

Knock-knock!

Who's there?

Tamara.

Tamara who?

Tamara you'll feel better
if you eat more fiber.

**Did you hear about the dentist
who diagnosed his patient's bad breath?**

The patient was in the waiting room
at the time.

**Why did the doctor prescribe
acne medication to the teenager?**

Because he was seeing spots.

**Why did the dumb guy bring
a chair to his doctor?**

They said he needed to
bring in a stool sample.

Did you hear about the guy who went to Costco and then went to the doctor?

First, he got free samples, and then he left pee samples.

Did you know the residents of Belgium have some of the worst allergies in the world?

They're all Phlegmish.

Which nut has the worst allergies?

Ca-shew!

Did you hear about the guy who had a massive waxy buildup in his head?

It was earful, just earful!

What do mean girls do to dandruff?

Give it the cold shoulder.

PATIENT: Doctor, I'd like to treat my hemorrhoids. Do you have any articles or research I can read?

DOCTOR: Piles!

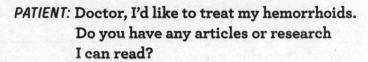

PATIENT: Doctor, I think I need glasses.

MAN: I agree. This is a toilet store.

PATIENT: What did you think of my urine sample?

DOCTOR: Frankly, it was pee-utiful.

WOMAN: Doctor! My husband's farts smell like fish, and I can't stand it!

DOCTOR: What a poor sole!

PATIENT: Doctor, my nose won't stop running.

DOCTOR: Just let it keep at it. It will tire itself out soon.

Did you hear about the girl
with too much earwax?
It was downright ear-ie.

What did the doctor say to the witch?
Wart's up?

A proctologist goes out to dinner one night, and a waiter comes to take his order. He notices the waiter keeps scratching his butt. The proctologist asks, "Do you have hemorrhoids?" The waiter replies, "We've only got what's on the menu."

Why did the rooster call in sick?
He had the cock-a-doodle-flu.

Why did the bowel movement
go to the doctor?
It was always pooped.

**Did you hear about
the lactose-intolerant comedian?**

He's great; none of his jokes is cheesy.

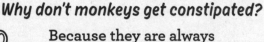

Why don't monkeys get constipated?

Because they are always
in the swing of things.

Why did the clarinet player smell so bad?

She was always practicing her wind instrument.

What dog has the most germs?

A bac-terrier.

**What do you get when
a cat has a cold?**

Mew-cus.

PATIENT: Doctor, I haven't pooped in weeks.

DOCTOR: Well, don't just sit there!

✚

PATIENT: Doctor! could you please treat my toad?

DOCTOR: No. I'm afraid if I touch it, it will croak.

✚

PATIENT: Doctor! I think I'm gonna hurl!

DOCTOR: What have you eaten today?

PATIENT: I've eaten two red licorices, three yellow taffies, and four blue ribbon candies.

DOCTOR: It's no wonder! You haven't been getting enough greens.

✚

PATIENT: Doctor, my feet keep falling asleep!

DOCTOR: Try wearing louder shoes.

What is another name for snowman dandruff?

Frosted Flakes.

Hard-of-hearing Harold and his loud wife Joan went to the doctor. "I am going to need a urine and feces sample," the doctor said. To which Joan yelled, "HAROLD, HE NEEDS A PAIR OF YOUR UNDERWEAR!"

What's the best part about flossing your teeth?

Finding all the free snacks for later!

What do you leave for a waiter whose ears are full of gunk?

A Q-tip.

What do zits drink?

Pop.

What should you never eat if a person with dandruff gives it to you?

A powdered doughnut.

An old woman went to the doctor's office. "Doctor," she said in a raspy voice, "I have an issue with gas. I fart, but they're silent and never smell. How can you help me?" "Well," the doctor said, "Take one of these every morning." He handed the small bottle of pills to the lady. Next week, the lady came back and said, "Doctor! Now my farts smell horrible! What did you give me?" "Good, good. Now that your sinuses are clear, let's work on your hearing."

What do Italian teenagers eat?

Zit-i.

Why should you not worry when you get a pimple?

Because zit happens.

**What's the difference between
a banana and a pimple?**

One bruises easily, the other oozes easily.

**I remember when
my ears used to be a lot filthier.**

Sorry, I was just waxing nostalgic.

**Why didn't anyone want to hang
out with Dandruff Dave?**

He was really flaky.

What do you call a little zit?

A simple pimple.

**What do you get from
a nauseated cow?**

Spoiled milk.

Have you heard the one about the constipated lion?

Get ready to roar!

Why was the pig covered in pimples?

It forgot to use medicated oinkment.

Why did the pig farmer go to the hospital?

He caught a bad case of pink eye.

What dessert should a proctologist never bring to a potluck?

Chocolate cream pie.

Did you hear about the kid who had really smelly armpits?

His teacher gave him a D because he never raised his hand in class.

PATIENT: Doctor, these fart pills don't help at all! I'm still tooting.

DOCTOR: Which end did you put them in?

✚

PATIENT: Doctor, how do I get my nose to stop running?

DOCTOR: Stick your foot out and trip it!

✚

PATIENT: Doctor! People say my farts sound like a motorbike!

DOCTOR: You shouldn't let them rev you up.

✚

PATIENT: Doctor, I've got uncontrollable diarrhea. What should I do?

DOCTOR: Wear brown pants.

PATIENT: Doctor, you gotta help me! I eat apples, I see apples in the toilet later. I eat bananas, and nothing but bananas comes out.

DOCTOR: Have you tried eating poop?

✚

PATIENT: Doctor, I got a case of diarrhea!

DOCTOR: Take it out of the case, for goodness' sake!

✚

PATIENT: Doctor! I fart so loudly I keep myself awake at night!

DOCTOR: You should sleep in another room.

✚

PATIENT: Help, doctor, my daughter just swallowed a pen! What should I do?

DOCTOR: Well, you probably aren't going to want to use that pen anymore.

What was the constipated librarian doing in the bathroom?
Working on the backlog.

Fahrvergnügen: A German word that means "driving pleasure."
Fahrfrompüpen: A German word for constipation.

I tried to follow Constipation on Twitter but got blocked.

Why did the king stay on his throne?
He was constipated.

Did you hear about the author who couldn't poop for a week?

Talk about a bad case of writer's block.

Did you hear M. Night Shyamalan directed a movie about an impacted colon?

There was a twist at the end.

What soda tastes like prunes?

Dr. Pooper.

What did the rectum say was its relationship status on Facebook?

"It's constipated."

**What five words
can strike fear into the heart of
even the strongest, toughest brute?**

"Turn your head and cough."

**What flower do you give
someone who overcomes
constipation?**

A ploppie!

**Why was the decapitated head
so lonely?**

He had no body to be with.

**What do you get
if you cross a witch
with a constellation?**

Star Warts.

What's the difference between lice and dandruff?

Dandruff has almost no taste at all.

Knock-knock!

Who's there?

Sancho.

Sancho who?

Sancho a get-well card. How's your stomach feeling?

Why did the fleas leave the dirty, disgusting kid alone?

The lice had already called dibs.

Look, guys.
PMS jokes aren't funny.
Period.

PATIENT: Doctor! I have a problem! Every morning,
I poop at 7:00 on the nose!

DOCTOR: How is that a problem?

PATIENT: I get up at 9:00!

✚

PATIENT: I need a pill to help me stop sleepwalking.

DOCTOR: No. I'm afraid you need the exercise.

✚

PATIENT: Doctor! I need your help. I've only
pooped once in the last two weeks.

DOCTOR: You need to see a specialist—
Dr. Doodoolittle.

✚

DOCTOR: How have your bowel movements been?

PATIENT: Not great. The toilet's been broken, so I
don't go as much, and things are really
painful down there.

DOCTOR: Have you tried taking the plunger out of
the toilet?

One way to tell you've got bad breath:

You ask a friend for a piece of gum and they hand you a roll of toilet paper.

What did the gross magician say when he picked at his pimple?

Scabracadabra!

What do toenails and cheese have in common?

Their smell.

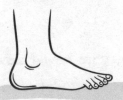

Whoever said "laughter is the best medicine" clearly never had diarrhea!

Did you hear about the really tall guy with dandruff?

The mayor thought it was snowing and canceled school for the day.

Why was the mathematician's bowel movement so upsetting?

Because it had a lot of problems.

Why did the environmentalist use so much mouthwash?

He wanted to fight air pollution.

Why was the ditch digger so constipated?

He was a mud clutcher.

Butt Wait, There's More!

BOOTY BUFFOONERY

What's the worst part about being a cowboy who rides around on a horse all day?

Rawhide.

Where do butts buy their groceries?

Hole Foods.

Why are only the cleanest butts allowed to sing solos?

Because they are soap-ranos.

What do you call an old butt that has seen it all?

A wise crack.

What soda do butts like best?

Squirt.

What do butts and lasers have in common?

They both go "pew-pew"!

How can you distinguish your dad's poop from others?

It's really corny.

Why did the turd never get anything done?

Because he was pooped.

What grows in the ground and smells like poo?

Turdnips.

Why did the guy get poop on his phone?

He was playing "Turds with Friends."

POO-PHEMISMS

- Baking brownies
- Crowning a new King of Brownland
- Checking in on breakfast
- I got an anaconda who don't wanna be in my buns, hon
- Wink at the toilet for an extended period of time
- Baiting the trap
- Bombing the porcelain sea
- Going to play Call of Doody
- Helping the beavers build a dam

*What did the butt cheeks say
after they lost the poop?*

"It's over between us!"

*Why did the
piece of poop
feel so old?*

Because he was
turning turdy.

*What do your bathroom and a bunch of
week-old bananas have in common?*

They're both ripe!

*What do you call an incompetent
accountant's bowel movement?*

An income poop.

Why did the kid bring a toilet to the birthday party?

He was a party pooper.

Knock-knock!

Who's there?

Freddy.

Freddy who?

Freddy or not,
I gotta go!

Why do underpants make good detectives?

Because they are good at going undercover.

What's the difference between a deep-fried wiener and a post-cookout poop?

One is a corn dog, and the other is a corned log.

POO-PHEMISMS

- Coaching the Browns
- Dropping the lobster in the water
- Drowning a rat
- Feeding the porcelain puppy
- Cutting bait
- Freeing the hostages
- Making mud pies
- Logging on
- Letting some air out of the tires
- Making a doo-posit
- Putting the meat loaf in the oven

What grows in the ground, smells like poo, and can be made into French fries?

Poo-tatoes.

What does Scooby-Doo do after eating Scooby Snacks?

Scooby doodie doo.

What's cute, furry, and eats cat poop?

A dog.

Did you hear about the guy that pooped in his sleep?

He took too many Tylenol BMs.

Why was the security guard
standing on dog poop?

He was on doody.

Why did the golfer
wear two pairs of pants?

In case she got a hole in one.

What's brown, smells horrid, and
got all over the horses and king's men?

Humpty's dump.

What do you call poop on a stick?

Shish-ka-poop.

How does poop surf the internet?

They log on.

Real Places that Sound Filthy

- Middelfart, Denmark
- Tooting Station, United Kingdom
- Drain, Oregon
- Blowhard, Australia
- Briny Breezes, Florida
- Atomic City, Idaho
- Greasy, Oklahoma
- Butteville, Oregon

What happened to the man who pooped on the sidewalk?

He was fined for littering.

What's tight, white, and full of holes?

Dad's underwear.

What did the pimple say to the butt?

"I'm tired of people picking on us!"

 ## What music band do butts like best?

Tom Petty and the Fart Breakers.

What do butts eat at the movies?

Poopcorn.

What does a competitive eater do in the bathroom?

Prepare for battle.

What did the guy get when he couldn't make it to the bathroom in time?

Heavy pants.

Knock-knock!

Who's there?

Iva.

Iva who?

Iva sore butt from that bathroom trip.

What do you get when you put a turd in the freezer?

A poopsicle.

DIRTY SLOGANS

Just what are these household brands trying to say?

"The Juice Is Loose" —STARBURST

"It Takes a Tough Man to Make a Tender Chicken" —PURDUE

"If It Doesn't Get All Over the Place, It Doesn't Belong on Your Face" —CARL'S JR.

"It Takes a Licking and Keeps on Ticking" —TIMEX

"It's Gonna Move Ya" —JUICY FRUIT

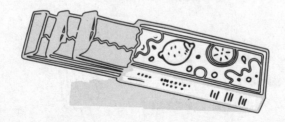

What's another name for panda poop?

Endangered feces.

What do you get after eating too many Oreos?

Cookie dookie.

Knock-knock!

Who's there?

Mop.

Mop who?

Stinks, huh?

Why did the pastry chef use jalapeños?

He wanted to ensure his buns were hot.

What do you get after eating too many blueberries?

Smurf poop.

What place did the piece of poop get in the race?

Turd place.

Why did the man poop on his lawn?

He was too cheap to buy fertilizer.

How is a butt like the Liberty Bell?

They both have a big crack.

What is another name for Eskimo poop?

Pudding Poops.

How do you get your butt to wipe itself?

Eat toilet paper.

More Real Places
that Sound Filthy

- Anus, France
- Bumpass, Virginia
- Colon, Michigan
- Tightsqueeze, Virginia
- Fanny, West Virginia
- Boody, Illinois
- Loose Creek, Missouri

**What do you call a poop
that comes out
really slooooooow?**
A turdle.

**What's worse than a big juicy fart
coming out of your butt?**
A big juicy fart going into your butt.

**Why did the cook wipe his butt
before he pooped?**
He liked to make things from scratch.

Knock-knock!
Who's there?
Butfor.
Butfor who?
Butfor pooping!

What did the guy say after he made a square poop?

"Ouch."

A bird in the hand will
probably poop in your hand.

What do dogs call rabbit poop?

Easter eggs.

What do you call poop you can't push out?

A frightened turtle.

---

*What do a spaceship and toilet
paper have in common?*

They both probe Uranus.

---

*What do dogs call it when they poop
in their crate?*

Midnight snack.

DIRTY SLOGANS

Just what are these household brands trying to say?

"What Can Brown Do for You?" —UPS

"Melts in Your Mouth, Not in Your Hand"
—M&Ms

"Plop, Plop, Fizz, Fizz. Oh, What a Relief It Is."
—ALKA SELTZER

"It's Finger-Licking Good" —KFC

"Is It Wet or Is It Dry?" —MR. CLEAN

"Once You Pop, You Can't Stop" —PRINGLES

What's another name for a poop that floats?

Bob.

What should you never order in a French restaurant?

Poofflé.

Have you seen Howard's End?

You probably shouldn't.
That's where his poop comes from!

What is the stinkiest palindrome?

POOP.

What's brown, sticky, and sounds like a clock tower?

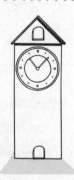

Dung.

How is your younger sibling like a diaper?
They're always full of it, and always on your butt.

Why shouldn't you buy shampoo?
It's fake. Get real poo.

Why was the boat embarrassed?
All the fish could see its bottom.

What do you get when you leave an old pair of underwear outside during a full moon?
An underwearwolf.

What gets better with age?
Dog poop.

What does Thor wear on his bottom?
Thunderpants.

Disgusting Titles Coming Soon to a Bookshelf Near You!

- *The Diarrhea Family*
  by Manny Luce-Bowles

- *Dealing with Constipation*
  by U. R. Stuck

- *How to Be a Proctologist*
  by Seymour Butz

- *How to Properly Clean Yourself*
  by Duke E. Viper

What do you call a fairy who's taking too long in the bathroom?

Stinkerbell.

How are socks like diapers?

They should be changed frequently.

JOHN: This bread is nice and warm.

BAKER: Should be. My cat's been sitting on it all morning.

Knock-knock!

Who's there?

Hallways.

Hallways who?

Hallways wash your hands when you go to the bathroom!

What does pig poop smell like?

It stoinks!

Knock-knock!

Who's there?

Snow.

Snow who?

Snow fun to go hiking
after eating too many prunes.

Why did the bum interrupt the speech?

Because he liked to butt in.

What do stinky kids eat for breakfast?

Poop Tarts.

How can you tell the difference between elephant and rhinoceros poop?

Elephants work for peanuts.

Why do lap dogs have the worst-smelling poop?

Because they are so spoiled.

Why do animals eat their meat raw?

Because they are terrible cooks.

Did you hear the joke about squirrel poop?

It was really nutty.

How many times a day does a composer poop?

Just once, but it takes four movements.

Why does toilet paper make a good detective?

It knows how to get to the bottom of things.

Knock-knock!

Who's there?

Pencil.

Pencil who?

Pencil fall down if you don't tighten your belt!

What's another name for cow poop?
Beef patties.

What does bear poop smell like?
Unbearable.

Why did the man leave the bathroom?
He turd enough of the stall next to him.

How did the toddler get such big muscles?

He was using Pull-Ups every night.

Knock-knock!
Who's there?
Europe.
Europe who?
No, you're a poo!

What is the most difficult animal to hold a conversation with?

A goat, because they always butt in.

What do a racetrack and your little brother's underwear have in common?

They're both covered in skid marks.

How do chickens know it's time to poop?

They use a cluck.

> *Knock-knock!*
>
> *Who's there?*
>
> *Haywood.*
>
> *Haywood who?*
>
> *Haywood you please pick up your dirty underpants off the bathroom floor?*

Knock-knock!

Who's there?

Chuck.

Chuck who?

Chuck your pants;
I think that fart went rogue.

Why did the cheetah eat the gazelle?

Because he loves fast food.

More Disgusting Titles Coming Soon to a Bookshelf Near You!

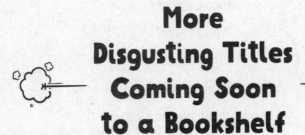

- *A History of Plumbers' Pants*
  by Sawyer Crack

- *How to Stop Vomiting*
  by Anya Neeze

- *The Most Frequent Urination Problems*
  by P.P. de Ponce

- *Common Rashes*
  by Mike Rauch-Burns

- *Chronic Gas*
  by Ran Sidass

*On which carnival ride is it okay
to poop your pants?*
The dumper cars.

What's brown and spins around your waist?
A hula poop.

What kind of pants can you poop in?
Dung-arees.

*What did Frankenstein
say after eating
the spicy burrito?*
Fire bad!

*What's worse than
finding fake poop in your bed?*
Finding real poop in your bed.

What do the poets do in the bathroom?

They write poo-ems.

What do you call a kid who crosses the road twice but refuses to take a bath?

A dirty double-crosser.

Why do ducks have tail feathers?

To cover their butt-quacks.

Why wouldn't the billionaire take a shower?

Because she was filthy rich.

What do baby mailmen deliver?

Diapers that are packed and loaded.